SLA | GUIDELIN

Open All Hours:
Out of Hours Learning
and the Secondary
School LRC

Fiona Devoy

Series Editor: Geoff Dubber

The School Library Association is an independent organisation and registered charity which was founded in 1937 to promote the development of libraries in schools. Today the SLA exists to support and encourage all those working in school libraries, raising awareness and promoting good practice through an effective training and publications programme. Membership of the Association brings many benefits including an advisory/information service for national and international enquiries, an excellent quarterly reviewing journal, and reduced rates for all publications and training courses. For full details, contact the SLA office in Swindon (address and telephone number below).

Acknowledgements

The author would like to thank Eileen Armstrong and Wendy Cooling for their helpful comments and suggestions. Thanks also to ContinYou for its kind permission to use the diagram on page five. (ContinYou was formed when the Community Education Development Centre and Education Extra merged on 14 October, 2003.)

Published by the School Library Association
Unit 2, Lotmead Business Village
Lotmead Farm, Wanborough
Swindon SN4 0UY
Tel: +44 1793 791787
Fax: +44 1793 791786
E-mail: publications@SLA.org.uk

© School Library Association 2004

Printed by Will Print, Oxford

Contents

HOMEWORK HELP?
Get extra help in the LRC
Mon & Tues   3.30-5.30
Wed   2.30-5.30
Ten top reasons for helping
yourself to Homework Help...
· Computers
· Internet access
· Staff support
· Expert advice
· Books to borrow for ideas
· Newspapers/magazines for research
· Photocopying
· Stationery supplies
· Space to study
· Loyalty card
Help yourself to a better grade!

'Whenever a library opens its doors it is offering study support.'[1]

In recent years the entire field of out of hours learning activities has expanded rapidly to embrace a wide range of exciting and challenging learning experiences going far beyond traditional homework and study clubs, even though these are still major players in the field. The interest in brain-based learning, the pressure to raise student attainment, the Government's interest in the field and the developing collection of research pointing to its success has all contributed to its expansion.

Research as far back as June 2000 showed that:

'Ninety-seven per cent of schools are now providing out of school hours learning activities… A typical primary school pupil is spending nearly two hours a week and a secondary school pupil three hours a week on out of hours learning. Fifty-four per cent of schools are planning to introduce further activities…'[2]

This Guideline aims to mirror this growth of events and expand on Jenny Cottrell's earlier SLA publication.[3] Although many of the principles are the same – the focus is still very much on the learner and voluntary informal learning – the opportunities and variety of experiences are now much wider; ranging from breakfast clubs to reading clubs to summer schools. This publication aims to put the range of possibilities into perspective for the school librarian, and highlight the potential role of Library Resource Centre (LRC) staff in this kaleidoscope of activities. Some of the theory behind the out of school activities movement is explained, and there are practical pointers for school library involvement in these exciting activities. Added value, not added burden, is the ideal, with the potential for the school librarian to have access to new resources, new ways of working and greater professional and personal satisfaction.

[1] DOUGLAS, J. Keynote presentation, SLG Conference, Cambridge, April 2002

[2] DfEE Research into school provision of out of hours learning activities www.qiss.org.uk/news/dfee_research.htm

[3] COTTRELL J. *Establishing a Homework Club in the Secondary School Library* (School Library Association, 1998) [No longer available]

'Out of school hours learning' is now an umbrella term for a range of activities that have burgeoned in schools in recent years. Appearing in many forms, it is any organised learning activity which takes place outside of the formal curriculum. This might be before school begins, at lunchtimes, after school ends, at weekends or during holiday periods. It needs to be emphasised that out of hours learning should not be confused with out of hours care, which, provided by many social services departments, is an extension to the school day for younger pupils who need to be looked after in the gap between the end of the school day and parents returning from work. While not denying that there may be learning opportunities for young people within this framework, the main thrust of this activity is care, not education, as it is when provided by education authorities and schools.

Also frequently referred to as 'study support', the term 'out of school hours learning', more accurately describes the wide range of activities on offer to students. Study support suggests, more narrowly, support for the academic aspects of the curriculum only, which does not describe accurately many of the opportunities on offer to young people today. Many activities which may, up until recently, only have been taking place because of the goodwill of teaching and support staff in schools, such as traditional sporting activities, or lunchtime clubs promoting a specific interest, now find they have been recognised as legitimate learning experiences, and may be eligible for funding from a variety of sources. The educational validity and the important contribution of these activities has now been recognised by the Government, and education authorities, as never before.

Why this comparatively recent development? Greater understanding of how students learn, combined with research into the value of less formal learning opportunities support the belief that individuals learn best when they can choose their own time and place to learn; when the emphasis is on less formal and more pleasurable ways of learning than in the usually more formal classroom setting. Despite the best efforts of caring and thoughtful classroom teachers, we all know that students' experience of learning outside the classroom can be very beneficial and help to create a more positive attitude towards school in general. A DfES report claimed that attending homework groups and other extra-curricular activities was likely to have the following impact on young people's learning:[4]

---

[4] MACBEATH, J. et al: *The Impact of Study Support* (DfES Research Report 273, 2001)

- improved exam results – up to 3.5 grades more on students' GCSE results[5]
- improved attendance rates in schools
- enhanced self-esteem and motivation to learn.

These benefits were held to be equally valid for both sexes, and the statistics showed that pupils from ethnic minorities or those who are socially disadvantaged benefited most from involvement in these programmes.

A study of the Tower Hamlets Study Support Project indicated that schools with programmes of study support showed an average thirty per cent increase in GCSE grades.[6]

Education Extra – now merged with Community Education Development Centre to become ContinYou[7] ('We provide advice, resources, information and support,' states its website.[8]) in England and Wales – and the Scottish Study Support Network, were appointed by the Government to identify and promote good practice across the country. The Code of Practice for Study Support identifies raising achievement as the main thrust of out of school hours learning, and provides the following framework for understanding how the wide range of activities, which contribute to study support, fit together:

- activities that **enable**, and help pupils to develop basic and key skills
- activities that **extend** the scope of the formal curriculum, building on existing class-based activities
- activities that **enrich** pupils' experience, providing new opportunities for learning.[9]

[5] See www.qiss.org.uk/main.htm

[6] Quoted in OFSTED report, *Learning Out of Hours: the Quality and Management of Study Support in Secondary Schools* (E-publication. HMI 466, October 2002)

[7] See www.educationextra.org.uk

[8] op. cit

[9] MACBEATH J. *Code of Practice: Study Support* (The Quality in Education Centre, University of Strathclyde, 1997)

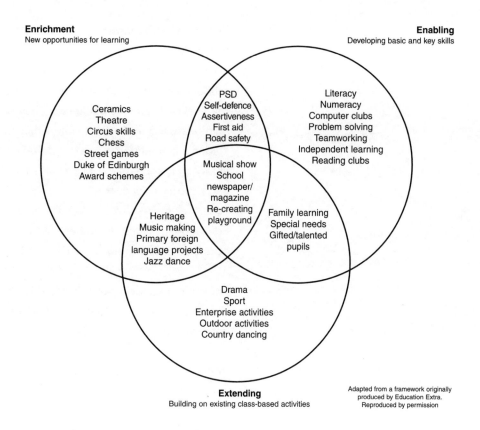

Enrichment
New opportunities for learning

Enabling
Developing basic and key skills

Ceramics
Theatre
Circus skills
Chess
Street games
Duke of Edinburgh
Award schemes

PSD
Self-defence
Assertiveness
First aid
Road safety

Literacy
Numeracy
Computer clubs
Problem solving
Teamworking
Independent learning
Reading clubs

Musical show
School
newspaper/
magazine
Re-creating
playground

Heritage
Music making
Primary foreign
language projects
Jazz dance

Family learning
Special needs
Gifted/talented
pupils

Drama
Sport
Enterprise activities
Outdoor activities
Country dancing

Extending
Building on existing class-based activities

Adapted from a framework originally
produced by Education Extra.
Reproduced by permission

Out of school hours learning is especially valuable because it is voluntary. Young people must be voluntary partners in their own learning – they need to develop emotional involvement. These activities encourage them to develop independence, commitment and motivation, essential skills for all independent life-long learners. And because the activities are voluntary and free from the strictures of school, the students feel that they have greater control over their work.

An Exciting Role for Libraries and Library Staff

Reading this description of out of hours learning, many of us react, 'But we're already doing this!' Indeed many LRCs offer real and dynamic opportunities for study support. They are open to students outside of the school day; before school begins, at intervals and lunchtimes, and beyond the final bell, even at weekends. They provide a supportive atmosphere and understanding and expert staff within an informal learning setting in which students can reinforce or extend their classroom learning. Similarly, many library staff are already very involved in the provision of more organised extra-curricular activities, such as reading groups, or homework and computer clubs. Out of hours learning acknowledges and formalises the educational validity of all these activities and also, in many cases, offers possibilities of additional funding and resources to support and extend them.

LRCs are in an ideal position when the role and management of out of hours learning in a school setting is considered. As Jonathan Douglas[10] has commented:

'Study support offers an exciting role for the school librarian. The enrichment and extension of the learning experience is the purpose of study support and is the very essence of the school librarian's role. What setting within the school is better for the creation of independent learners than the library?'[11]

The most obvious activities, for which most school library staff are happy to offer provision and support, are in the areas of study support for homework, literacy and ICT, and also in developing and honing study, revision and exam preparation skills. They can also play a major role in developing effective learning/information handling skills and in raising pupils' awareness of their own learning styles and techniques.

On a less formal note, out of hours learning also offers school library staff opportunities to step out of their traditional role and to share their own passions and hobbies with students. Out of hours learning is not restricted to study support, academic and curriculum-based pursuits, but is also intended to enrich the life experience of students who might otherwise never have the opportunity to experience a range of specialist activities and interests. If the maths teacher can become involved in football coaching through out of hours pursuits, then we librarians can also step out of role and enthuse young people with our own passions and hobbies. If theatre or opera appreciation or performance, quilting, horse riding, climbing, motorcycling or even white-water rafting is your particular thing, then get involved!

10 Formerly CILIP's Advisor on Youth and Schools

11 DOUGLAS, J. 'Study Support; why it matters', *School Libraries In View*, Spring 2002 (16) p.11

This involvement in an LRC setting or beyond will help develop library staff relationships across the school and reduce that sense of isolation. It will improve the status of the LRC and the postholder and help to strengthen understanding with students and other adult colleagues.

A major principle of out of hours learning promoted by ContinYou is that tutors should be selected for their appropriateness, from the wider community, not just from within the teaching staff of the school.[12] For example, in one primary school, a classroom assistant who is also a native French speaker, is tutor for a conversational French club. In another, a parent who is a qualified sports coach runs the football club. To quote a headteacher from one school:

'I was very clear about the kind of people we wanted as tutors. We drew up a job description that put the emphasis on relationships, getting on well with kids, openness to learning along with them... It is important not to offend or exclude staff, but we also have to be clear about the blend and range of expertise, whose interests we are serving, and what would be most likely to achieve our goals.'[13]

Library staff are not only the obvious but also often the favoured candidates with their knowledge of the students, the resources and also the curriculum.

Out of hours learning, therefore, will offer opportunities to become involved, on a voluntary basis, in less formal learning situations, and can provide a positive benefit to LRC staff and contribute to their continuing professional development.

[12] MACBEATH, J. op cit, p.18

[13] MACBEATH, J. op cit, p.19

Homework clubs

Out of hours learning can appear in many guises.[14]

These can operate in several different roles, with different targeted groups. Probably the most familiar form for clubs to take, and central to the work of LRC staff, are homework or study clubs. A quiet, comfortable and secure place to do their homework is what many students need – away from the distractions of home.

These clubs often create a natural extension to the school day, albeit less formal, for many students. They provide a quiet, comfortable and secure setting in which students can concentrate on homework away from the distractions of television, computer games, siblings, chores and the like. They offer easy access to quality school-based facilities, especially book and ICT resources frequently with clear and easy opportunities to consult with and work alongside adults who may well have specialist expertise. They usually provide a higher ratio of staff to pupils – one of the reasons for their success. Strong curriculum links between teaching and library staff are essential, however, if they are going to be successful. OFSTED noted the challenges:

'The majority of schools provide homework clubs. Their quality is variable. A common weakness is that those who run the activity have little idea of the nature of the homework set and no routine for feeding back to the teachers who set it. Attendance is rarely monitored. When it is, many schools find that those pupils who might benefit most are least likely to attend. Some schools are recognising the problem and targeting their provision at specific groups.'[15]

It is also important to have knowledge of the local homework club schemes run by the public library service. Public libraries provide very important and valuable homework and after school clubs for younger pupils and students, many involving organised groups of parents and mentors. In 1999 over 25 per cent of Library Authorities in England and Wales ran homework clubs.[16] Partnership rather than competition will be the way forward.

There are good example of homework clubs run jointly by local colleges and secondary schools and those that operate across the primary/secondary divide. The patterns of provision are many and varied.

---

[14] To see a variety of award-winning clubs see *Top Tips: Bright Ideas for Involving People from the Local Community in your Out of Hours Clubs* (Education Extra, 2003)

[15] *Learning Out of Hours* OFSTED report op. cit.

[16] BOTTEN, T. et al *Study Support; the Code of Practice for Public Libraries* (The Quality in Education Centre, University of Strathclyde, 1998)

Mentoring

This is another key development, supported by DfES initiatives which can link closely to LRC work in both primary and secondary schools. Adult and older students work with targeted younger students to build self confidence and self esteem, social skills and academic achievement. Listening and communication skills can be honed. Issues as diverse as bullying, access to university and other higher education courses, industry and commerce can be addressed and support given to catch up on missed work or homework.

'Initially it was thought that teachers would help, but we have appointed a core of "Sixth Form Mentors". They are some of our Sixth Form students who are paid to help younger pupils with homework difficulties. Curriculum Co-ordinators (staff who have curriculum responsibilities for an individual year group) identify pupils who need support and these pupils are the Mentors' main responsibility... the Mentors are under my jurisdiction and will also carry out other library duties as I request.'[17]

Pupil mentoring is widely accepted as a powerful method of developing inclusion and school ethos.[18] However, some authorities, while happy to have pupils as volunteer mentors, may have a policy of non-payment for this commitment.

The National Mentoring Network provides a range of advice and leaflets.[19] The LRC can provide a welcoming and secure environment for this work and both mentor and mentee can take advantage of the resources on offer. OFSTED comments:

'Where provided, mentoring of pupils is good in two out of five schools and helps to improve confidence and motivation. In over half the schools using mentors, the evidence suggests they have an impact on examination results. Where there are weaknesses... they usually arise from unclear aims, inadequate briefing or lack of continuity in contact.'[20]

After school clubs and the associated mentoring or peer mentoring support may well go beyond the homework opportunity and here again the LRC can be a very useful venue.

Reading clubs

Many schools, usually through the LRC, now offer reading clubs, either in lunchtimes or after school, for a mixture of students and/or adults.

---

[17] Message sent to the school librarian network listserv, 2002

[18] www.aude-education.co.uk/mentoring.htm

[19] www.nmn.org.uk

[20] *Learning Out of Hours* OFSTED report op. cit

The opportunities and activities are limitless, depending only on the time, resources, ingenuity and enthusiasm of LRC staff. One excellent club is that run in Southwold School, Nottingham, a Language and Community School.[21] Started in 1999 the club now caters for 25–30 Y7 students each week. Teaching staff are involved alongside the librarian and the goodwill and social interaction are as important as the clear appreciation of reading and books. Existing initiatives, such as the shadowing scheme for the CILIP Carnegie and Kate Greenaway Medals, can help to gain funding.

Computer clubs

ICT-based clubs may well naturally find a home in the LRC, if not in the school's ICT suite. The links between computer literacy and information literacy are clear and LRC staff can often suggest another dimension to screen work or can provide an ICT context for other activities – story writing, book reviews, interactive games, revision tests, etc. For the younger age range, children aged 7–11, The GridClub initiative is excellent. Created in August 2001 in England and Wales, and supported by DfES funds of £6 million by July 2003, it is now also available in Scotland.[22] This provides a free high quality on-line service to registered schools where younger pupils can access a range of resources and services safely over the Internet. Holding computer club activities in the LRC demonstrates the importance of the LRC, reminds users of the links with other resources and provides that essential ingredient – LRC staff to demonstrate the links, provide ideas of other websites and act as the knowledge manager as information queries arise and need answering.

Dads 'n' lads

There are now many Dads 'n' Lads groups around the UK, many with a sporting focus, but others with a library connection. The Literacy Trust website provides examples of clubs run in Bedworth, Islington, Doncaster, Hampshire and Bradford.[23] They are a fund of ideas – see also the local Dads 'n' Lads site run in the Melton district of Leicestershire.[24] There are real possibilities for LRCs in these ventures.

Revision clubs

Targeted at exam classes these are frequently offered for a short time only in the run-up to the actual examinations. Here again the LRC can offer its resources and accommodation. LRC staff can provide revision guides, copies of past papers and past coursework and put on displays of information literacy techniques – essay writing, note taking, etc to support this work.

[21] 'Running a school reading club – ideas from the "front line"' by Wrighton, S. in *School Libraries In View*, Autumn 2002 (17)

[22] www.gridclub.com

[23] www.literacytrust.org.uk, see Reading the Game, a section of the website

[24] http://homepage.ntlworld.com/paulfleming

Study clubs

Often with a specific subject focus – perhaps archaeology, history, geology, science, technology, music, maths, art, etc – these clubs interest students and are sometimes run by subject teaching staff. Here again links to the LRC to use book and ICT resources and the LRC itself as a venue are clear.

Easter and summer schools

These are held outside term time as the names suggest, and will support a number of age ranges. Easter schools are usually aimed at the upper years of secondary school, and linked to revision clubs. They are planned to provide extra subject tuition, help and advice on exam and study techniques for pupils about to sit national examinations. The venue may be the students' own school – often the LRC, although to provide variety, relief and to build community partnership the local college of further education with its differing facilities may be used.

Summer schools again are held in a variety of venues – secondary schools, colleges of further and higher education, or universities. Their focus may be primary–secondary transition or improving literacy or numeracy skills. Working with those students about to enter secondary school presents an ideal opportunity for library staff to get to know these newcomers before term begins, and introduce them to the LRC in a fun way before the formal curriculum takes over.[25] Alternatively, these clubs may encourage older students to think about applying for higher education or perhaps provide taster courses in specific activities or studies. There are many possibilities for school librarians to be involved in these clubs, either in or beyond their own school, more so if the activities have a core skills – literacy or ICT – focus.

Breakfast and lunchtime clubs

Breakfast clubs generally focus on the sound principle that students work best when they have had a nutritious meal before school starts. There is potential for a study element to these, and it may be very beneficial opening the LRC early to support this kind of initiative. 'Early bird' tutors can be employed to support homework activities and school library services may well be very happy to provide extra resources especially for a reading corner or school library that encourages pupils to use any free time they have in a worthwhile way.

Lunchtime clubs can provide many of the kinds of activities carried out in after school clubs, and these are often more popular to pupils who live at a distance. The feasibility of lunchtime activities may depend on the configuration of the school day in a particular establishment, whether there are staggered lunchtimes, and what the existing opening hours are.

---

[25] See *Library Induction: Introducing Students and Staff to the Secondary School Library* (School Library Association, 2001)

Residential experiences

These can take the form of study weekends for senior pupils or activities weekends for other age groups. Again library staff, with their specialist knowledge of the resources, would be excellent for tutoring or as an adult helper.

Linking with partner schools, colleges and universities

Creating links with partner primary schools can effectively involve out of hours activities and clubs. Many secondary schools invite older primary age children from neighbouring schools – the extension of out of hours activities is obvious. Exciting activities and a new range of skills and facilities is often a draw to these younger children.[26] At the other end an after school club can offer opportunities to see and perhaps experience further and higher education in its different forms and guises.

[26] DEVOY, F. 'If we enjoy it, does it mean we're not learning?' in Dubber, G. *The Internet, the Primary School Library and the Independent Learner* (School Library Association, 2002)

'Inspection evidence continues to indicate that, where the activities are well focused and well run, they can significantly enrich pupils' experiences and improve their attitude to learning.'[27]

Before you start, have a think and a read! Suggested reading could include:

• The Quality in Study Support (QiSS) website – <www.qiss.org.uk/main.htm>. This provides ideas and guidance, gives advice on setting up and developing your contribution, explains how your achievements can be recognised and outlines QiSS's Professional Development Programmes.
• *The Essential Guide to the Impact of Study Support* (2002). Written by Tony Kirwan of QiSS, this provides simple guidance to schools.
• *The Code of Practice for Secondary Schools* (Revised 2000). This provides a clear framework of standards.
• *Learning Out of Hours: the Quality and Management of Study Support in Secondary Schools* (HMI 466).[28]

The opportunities are immense, depending on your own particular school and situation. If you want to become involved there are any number of options. Be clear, though, from the start that you have the time, commitment, school support and resources that you need. You might well have to look carefully at your job description – it may need amending, so too your job contract. You will need to ensure that extra staffing and resources are available so that the efficiency and effectiveness of all the other LRC services that you offer are not put at risk by your extra or changing role.

Payment arrangements will vary from authority to authority. In the best of situations, LRC staff may be paid an additional hourly rate, with no distinction from other professional staff. Some authorities will pay an overtime rate at the usual rate of pay. Some librarians may be happy to have an arrangement for time off in lieu of any additional hours worked. It is up to you to sort out what makes good sense for you and seems fair.

Key questions

Consider the following when planning what you and the LRC might offer:

• Is there a need for what you are thinking of providing? Is it being provided elsewhere in the school, or the wider community?
• What is the activity going to contribute to learning and raising achievement ? Clear aims and objectives will be needed for your bid.
• Can you sustain the commitment, both in terms of preparation time and

---

[27] *Learning Out of Hours* OFSTED report op. cit

[28] Available from www.ofsted.gov.uk/publications

time when the club is running? Clubs always need time and energy and good organisation. No one can possibly get involved in every initiative. If you are newly qualified or newly in post, is this the right time for you?

- Are other staff willing to be involved or will it all be dependent on you? There may be times due to sickness or out of school commitments when you will not be available.
- How many pupils will be interested/can you cope with? One of the major benefits for the students will be to work in smaller numbers in a calm non-classroom atmosphere. What do the students want? Do include quotes from them in your bid.
- Rather than starting afresh, can you obtain recognition and extra resourcing for what you are already doing? Developing your existing library club with its existing band of users might be better than starting something larger and grander.
- What are your plans for involving members of the local community?[29]
- What other practical arrangements might have to be made? For example catering, transport, caretaking, etc.
- Who provides the tea and biscuits and who pays for them?
- Will parental permission be needed?
- Will extra transport be required for pupils to get home and who pays?
- What plans do you have to measure the success of your activity?

Homework Club Questionnaire

An idea has been suggested to have a homework club: this is a short survey to give the librarian information on what you want.

1. Would you be interested in joining a homework club?

2. Where would be the best place to have the club. For example the LRC or the public library? Why?

3. What time/place should the homework club be on?

4. What equipment would you want available to you?

5. Would you rather it was a drop-in service or do you think you should be issued with pass cards? Why?

6. What helpers would you want to see? For example sixth form students, staff, library manager.

7. Would you want to use the computers? Why?

8. Any other comments?

Questionnaire produced by Cramlington Community High School (1997)

---

[29] See *Top Tips: Bright Ideas for Involving People from the Local Community in your Out of Hours Clubs* (Education Extra, 2003)

Creating and submitting your bid

Once you have decided on a specific activity, carried out some consultations and put together some possible costings, you may well need to prepare an official bid to secure permission, funding and recognition.

It is sensible to seek active support from your line manager, school study support co-ordinator and students at all stages of the process of creating and submitting a bid. It is then more likely to be successfully adopted by the senior management team who may themselves need to forward it the local education authority, depending on the scale of the planned activity.

If you have an ambitious and extensive plan involving the spending of several thousand pounds, this bid will probably be aimed directly at one of the major external fund-holders such as ContinYou. This will be more complicated, but help with this can be obtained from QiSS through its critical friends' project[30] or on the Charities Information Bureau website.[31] The information that the fund-holders require, whether in or beyond school, will be broadly similar.

It is important to establish links across the school, for your club – everyone should be a stakeholder and view the club as a whole school effort.

If it is going to be a homework club then remember the challenges outlined by OFSTED and quoted earlier:

'The quality is variable. A common weakness is that those who run the activity have little idea off the nature of the homework set and no routine for feeding back to the teachers who set it.'[32]

- What staffing levels will be needed and what training will staff, established or newly appointed, require to be effective?
- Don't be too ambitious in the first instance – let the club grow organically by word of mouth rather than attempting to attract large numbers which may be difficult to support and organise.
- Can you provide examples of the type of activities that you intend to include? For example use of new ICT software, revision techniques, use of educational board games, visits to the local library, major reference or university library, Record Office, etc.
- Have you costed the activities? It may be useful to provide separate figures for staffing resources, extra caretaking, utilities, etc.
- How do you intend to monitor and evaluate the success of your club?

---

30 www.qiss.org.uk/index.htm

31 www.cibfunding.org.uk

32 *Learning Out of Hours* OFSTED report op. cit

External funders will especially want to know that their money is being used wisely to support clear educational objectives.

Large sums of money have been made available to support out of hours learning, directly from the Government and through special project funding from ContinYou, the charity set up in 1992 as Education Extra to develop out of hours learning activities and channel funding. Education Extra Cymru (now ContinYou Cymru) was launched in Wales in 2001. Over the ten years since its conception, ContinYou has been able to give over £3 million in grants to schools, in partnership with other organisations such as The Paul Hamlyn Foundation (reading clubs), Kellogg's (breakfast clubs) and Deutsche Bank (maths clubs).[33] In 2001 ContinYou was awarded the DfEE (now DfES) contract to run the Diana Princes of Wales Memorial Award for Young People, rewarding achievement among young people across the UK.

Millions of pounds of funding has been directed to out of hours learning, initially, from 1991 to 1999, through the Prince's Trust, a charity set up by the Prince of Wales to help people aged 14–30 to reach their full potential. The Trust set up 314 new study clubs in 2002–2003.[34] Funding from them for further development work is available. Funding was also allocated by the Government through the National Lotteries Board, firstly through the Excellence Fund (£27 million from 1998–2001 in Scotland), then through the New Opportunities Fund (over £23.6 million from 2002 for three years). This funding has been allocated to LEAs and then forwarded to schools, so if you are seeking funding beyond the school, then your initial request for funding should still be made to your school management team and governors.

Running your club

There is no shortage of advice for library staff dealing with the practicalities of running an out of hours event.

Membership of ContinYou costs £30 for secondary schools and £20 for primary schools. This will provide support in a number of formats – termly magazines, newsletters, advice over the phone, access to professional development and training opportunities, and reduced price on a number of publications. Especially to be recommended are the excellent publications in the 'How To…' range.[35] These packs give practical advice on running a variety of clubs. Similarly, the publication *Top Tips* gives lots of practical advice from the organisers of clubs already running.[36]

---

[33] *Creating that Extra Chance: Annual Report 2001–2002* (Education Extra, 2002)

[34] www.princes-trust.org.uk

[35] *How to Run a Successful Reading Club* (Education Extra)

[36] *Top Tips: Bright Ideas for Running Successful Out of Hours School Clubs*, (Education Extra, 2002) Available online at www.educationextra.org.uk

Network with other LRC managers in your local SLS, SLA branch and area to discover those already involved in exciting out of hours projects. Visit them to see their activities in action.

Useful tips

Consider the following useful tips:

- Attract students by:
    - individual invitation
    - a special launch event
    - open invitation – talking with students in small groups, class time or at assemblies.

You will need to outline exactly what you are offering, to whom and when and explain the benefits to them! Your enthusiasm, commitment and promotional skills will be your key selling points!

- Establish an upper limit of numbers (even if this is discussed only with colleagues in the first instance). It really is important to give the firstcomers the care and attention that they need and expect.

- Keep an accurate register of attendance. This safeguards you with the attendance of individual students – you know who came along on a specific occasion and it clearly indicates overall numbers of users and trends. Giving out stickers and operating a reward system is a common way of rewarding regular attendance and usually works quite well.

- Be very careful to operate your school's Health and Safety and Child Protection policies and procedures.

- Involve other adults – this shares the load and provides some flexibility to you.

- With any club good time keeping is important. Parents, carers or siblings may be waiting or students have to rush off to lessons or jobs. With an after school club – especially with younger pupils, ensure everyone is collected or has left the premises before you yourself leave.

- Organise a natural break from the formal school day – at lunchtime or after school. Provide refreshments before study begins, or at lunchtime give the students time to eat their lunch – even in the library!

- If you are supporting homework, then make sure you know the context of the homework and have a clear understanding of the curriculum requirements.

- Organise feedback for curriculum staff on the tasks completed, and progress made, by individual students.

- Keep the time and place consistent. The activity may lose momentum if changes are made. Regular attendance will be encouraged by regular happenings.

- Make attendance straightforward for students. You may need to make special arrangements for them for a lunchtime club – perhaps the provision of passes to get into the dinner hall early or special arrangements for late travel home after school.

- Use bribery – it usually works! Give prizes for regular attendance and/or clear evidence of improved attainment, commitment, behaviour, etc – cinema tickets, tickets to football matches or other sporting events, tokens for CDs, books, etc. (Some of these could be sponsored.)
- Relax the usual rules by, for example, allowing pupils to eat in the library, but don't let normal discipline slide. The atmosphere may be more informal, but common sense and good behaviour should be the norm.
- Organise special events occasionally, and invite teaching colleagues, support staff and adults from outside school to come along. For example authors, librarians from SLS, and parents, local celebrities, etc.
- Encourage students to become involved in the organisation and planning of the club or range of activities. One feature of effective practice is that pupils' views are sought and they play a strong part in designing the programmes.[37]
- Borrow ideas from colleagues and other professionals. If you are running a reading club, consider joining the Reading Club Network.[38]
- Hook pupils at the end of one session by telling them what will be happening next session/week.
- Involve club members in creating and distributing publicity material.
- Show that you're caring and sharing – that you know the curriculum and you can help them with their tasks or to learn new skills or experiences.
- Don't be afraid to repeat popular activities, especially if you have been too busy to plan something new.
- With their permission, display items that students might produce.
- Invite your line manager, Head and local study support co-ordinator to see the exciting and challenging activities that are organised and operated. Remember to invite them to special events which have been organised.
- Have an awards ceremony at the end of the year. Celebrate the students' achievements. You may be able to do this at the school's awards ceremony, or at a whole school assembly.

Do talk to colleagues and your line manager about any difficulties. If you are finding it difficult to attract students, then maybe the timing is wrong. Students who travel some distance may not wish to stay after school, the club may clash with another attractive option. Workload/coursework may be too heavy at that time. If you have any specific difficulty, remember too that another librarian somewhere is likely to have the same problem. Talk with your SLS, your local SLA branch or post a message onto a newsgroup.[39] Advice is never far away.

---

[37] *Learning Out of Hours* OFSTED report op. cit

[38] www.readingclub.org.uk

[39] The school librarian network listserv is a good example – sln-subscribe@yahoo.groups.com

Measuring your success

Everyone will want to know about and celebrate your success, even if you are operating within existing budgets, resources and buildings. As the club/activity organiser you will need to evaluate your success, not only to reassure yourself but also to share it with your students, parents, school colleagues, the community and sponsors or fund holders.

Gather information from:
- registers of attendance and planning/summary notes of the activities
- questionnaires to the students to assess their attitudes towards the club and their new learning, to school colleagues to demonstrate the difference you're making, to parents

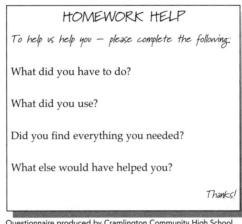

HOMEWORK HELP

To help us help you – please complete the following:

What did you have to do?

What did you use?

Did you find everything you needed?

What else would have helped you?

Thanks!

Questionnaire produced by Cramlington Community High School

- photographs of pupils involved in activities – make sure you obtain permission to do this from your line manager and the students
- comments noted by you in your LRC logbook
- value-added scores on attainment tests conducted before and after club involvement
- staff assessments of these pupils' attitudes and attainment
- opinions of staff who work alongside you in the club/or activity and how they feel their participation has added to their own continuing professional development
- student diaries or video diaries
- competition entries
- comments from the Education Welfare Service, Social Services, etc.

This evidence will be used to show that the students are getting better at:
- learning
- organising themselves
- time keeping
- interaction with others
- attending regularly.

It will also show itself by an increase in students' performance through:

- self confidence and self esteem
- higher attainment.

Clearly, attendance is the crudest measure of success, as all attendance is voluntary, and students will obviously not attend if your offer and range of activities does not appeal to them!

A useful publication is *Outcomes of Out of School Hours Learning: A Framework for Analysis*. It provides an overview of the range of possible positive outcomes that out of school activities can provide.[40]

---

[40] *Outcomes of Out of School Hours Learning: A Framework for Analysis* (Education Extra, 2002) Available online at www.educationextra.org.uk

Even the most misfitting child
Who chanced upon the library's worth,
Sits with the genius of the Earth
And turns the key to the whole world.[41]

The evidence for the benefits of out of hours learning appears overwhelming. The range of activities that have sprung up is quite phenomenal. Out of hours learning, in its many different guises, is now a recognised activity in thousands of secondary schools. My own involvement in out of school hours learning, in both primary and secondary schools, has been very positive. And it has given me opportunities for personal and professional development that I would not otherwise have had. I have also been amazed at the variety of activities on offer in the schools I have visited, providing experiences which I am sure have enriched the social and learning experiences of the children and students who have taken part.

Out of hours learning can provide the school librarian, as an organiser, as a tutor or mentor with opportunities to learn alongside students, and to offer learning experiences, encouragement and commitment which may not otherwise have been possible within the more rigid and crowded formal curriculum and working day.

'As the school's expert in information and learning skills, skills which empower the student as a lifelong learner, the school librarian is the natural champion of study support.'[42]

An opportunity, in my opinion, too good to be missed!

---

[41] HUGHES, TED 'Hear It Again', July 1997

[42] DOUGLAS J. op cit.

Case Study 1
RAP sessions @ Saltley School, Birmingham

Karen Gilchrist, LRC Manager, Saltley School, Birmingham; with
Sharon Woolley, LRC Assistant Manager, and Fadl Hadi, Out of Hours
Learning Co-ordinator
11–16 Comprehensive, 920 students

Background

The Learning Resource Centre at Saltley School is open for approximately fifty hours per week. We are open two nights a week until 6.30pm and also for two hours on a Saturday morning. The LRC is staffed by a professional librarian and a library assistant. We receive direct support from an out of hours learning co-ordinator. As a professional librarian I am delighted to see the school's commitment to out of hours learning. During the four years that the LRC staff have been in post out of hours learning has become a central feature of LRC work and has proved itself to be of great benefit to the pupils.

The out of hours learning sessions are called RAP, which is an acronym for 'Raising Achievement Project'. The emphasis during these sessions is placed on coursework, homework and revision. Evening sessions, held twice a week, 4.30–6.30pm, focus on supporting Y10 and Y11 study. For two hours each session the pupils have a dedicated teacher, learning support assistant, whenever available, and a member of the library staff working with them. With the addition of fifteen computers with Internet access and various Microsoft applications, together with a wide range of up-to-date stock that complements the curriculum, the pupils have a wealth of information at their fingertips.

On Saturdays during term time RAP takes place from 10–12pm. This session is primarily aimed at Y7, Y8 and Y9 pupils, although Y10 and Y11 are very welcome to attend. On average between thirty and forty pupils attend these RAP sessions. Much to our delight, with the increasing popularity of this extra learning opportunity attendance figures are steadily increasing and we have seen as many as seventy pupils come along! As with the evening sessions dedicated members of staff are at hand to assist the pupils in their task but we do encourage the youngsters to work by themselves or in pairs or small groups when possible – encouraging independent learning!
A librarian is available on Saturdays too – usually fully briefed by the teachers about the current homework tasks given to the pupils.

Promotion

RAP starts in September each year. It is promoted throughout school by senior management, heads of year, teachers, the out of hours co-ordinator and LRC staff. More encouragingly, pupils talk to each other and the most persuasive advertisement is word of mouth. RAP continues throughout the year. There are times when numbers fluctuate (religious events and parents evenings for example) but generally these stay at an average of 100–150 visits per week for the evening RAP sessions. These figures usually increase during the spring and summer terms in the lead up to exams. Although it is mainly Y11s who attend these sessions we do start to encourage Y10 pupils in the summer term. This encourages regular attendance of RAP sessions before starting in Y11.

Pupils who attend RAP must fill out a parental permission form. This lists any medical conditions and has an emergency contact number should we need to get in touch with parents or carers at any time. We expect the same standard of behaviour during the out of hours sessions to that of the school day. A member of staff is present in the main entrance foyer of the school to supervise pupils entering and leaving the building. Pupils must sign a register on entry and also in the LRC, this is to ensure the staff know the whereabouts of pupils at all times. During evening and Saturday sessions a head count is taken for extra security.

Challenges

During the last four years we have built up an excellent relationship with pupils. However, there have been some challenges. These usually occur when new pupils attend RAP and are unfamiliar with the working ethos; sometimes induction is needed to establish standard practices of behaviour. Pupils quickly become aware that RAP is not a social club but a highly effective working and learning environment.

RAP has made a valuable contribution to improved exam results across the school. In 1999–2000 approximately a quarter of the students who attended RAP on a regular basis attained five or more A–C passes. This is just one of the benefits of RAP. Pupils are proud of their regular attendance to the sessions and are pleased when they have completed a particularly challenging piece of homework or coursework, which, in turn builds their self-esteem.

Our out of hours learning sessions are successful because of several key factors, including:
• support from senior management
• committed and dedicated staff
• the out of hours learning co-ordinator
• good facilities
• parental support
• enthusiastic pupils.

From a librarian's perspective our role is to assist pupils in finding relevant and useful information from either books or multimedia applications. This is especially important when pupils are completing coursework. The librarian's skill at teaching and promoting research and information handling skills is a valuable resource. An example of this was recently demonstrated when two pupils were looking for a picture of the interior of a church, with the supporting information, for their religious education homework. They were having difficulty finding what they needed on the Internet so, they asked for advice. The librarian guided the pupils to the appropriate books and they were able to find the precise information in the minimum time enabling them to complete the task and move on to other work. They learned the important lesson that the Internet isn't always the quickest or most effective information source!

Recognition

As a librarian I am proud that Saltley School's Learning Resource Centre has the essential components needed to be the effective venue for the school's RAP sessions. It is also rewarding for LRC staff to work with pupils from all years in an out of hours environment. RAP has greatly increased the recognition of the LRC as a vital information source and a cross-curricular study area.

Helen Hale, Librarian, Melbourn Village College, Cambridgeshire
11–16 Comprehensive, 560 students

Background

Melbourn Village College is an 11–16 comprehensive school serving a number of villages in a rural part of South Cambridgeshire. It has 560 pupils. The school was considered very favourably in its most recent OFSTED inspection four years ago. The Village Colleges in Cambridgeshire have a strong tradition of community links.

The Library Resource Centre is a bright attractive room in the centre of the school site and is heavily used in school time by several subject departments who book in classes, or send down groups and individuals from lessons. I have been in post just over five years and have built up links with teaching and support staff especially in the area of information skills teaching.

There are around 9000 items in the LRC, including books, audiotapes, newspaper cuttings and CD-ROMs. There are six computers for student use, five are linked to the school curriculum network and have access to the Internet, the Library catalogue (ALICE), CD-ROMs and Microsoft Office software. The sixth computer is a standalone that is used for CD-ROMs and word processing.

The LRC is staffed by me – a Chartered Librarian, working part time and a part-time Library Assistant. Between us we cover the whole school day including lunchtimes and breaks, and also two homework club sessions per week. We have a small amount of overlap time, but this is mostly at lunchtimes in order to manage student numbers at this busy time and to give me time to eat my lunch!

MVC homework club

Our Homework Club started around five years ago. The LEA invited us to submit an application to participate in a pilot scheme funded by the New Opportunities Fund (NOF). Since then we have received NOF money through its Out of School Hours Learning Programme. Different LEAs organise their out of hours activities differently within the NOF requirements.

The LRC was the obvious place in the school to hold the club, as it is a large enough room, it is attractive and comfortable, and has in stock sufficient books and computers together in one room for students to comfortably and easily use. We welcomed the involvement and the chance to add the LRC dimension to our students' work. In our submission, part of our 'target audience' was students living in rural villages with no access to public libraries and no computers at home to support their homework. Funding still comes from NOF via the LEA, and we have to feed back data on attendance, etc, to the LEA on a quarterly and annual basis. There is a revenue grant which pays for the staffing of the club and resources (stationery, books, software, ICT) and a small initial capital grant for equipment for the club to use. We have to renew our bid periodically, as NOF grants usually only run for three years.

The club is co-ordinated by the Head of Y7, who has responsibility for the induction of the new intake Y7 students and the development of their learning and study skills. She liaises with parents and the LEA, and with relevant staff within school such as the Learning Support Co-ordinator and us busy LRC staff. The Bursar liaises with the LEA on the financial aspects of the initiative. There are two sessions each week, on Wednesdays and Thursdays to fit in around school meeting timetables, and sessions run for around an hour each, after school but with a short 'comfort' break between school ending and the club starting. Club sessions are staffed by a teacher with the support of a Learning Support Assistant and a member of the library staff.

Improving study habits

We decided to concentrate on younger students and link club practice to developing good homework and study habits for newer students to the College. Hence Y7 and Y8 students are invited (by a letter sent home to all parents in September) to sign up for club sessions, usually one but sometimes both each week, and students who need learning support or have a difficult home situation are particularly encouraged to come along. There are around twenty students each session. Regular attendance is expected and casual drop-in use is not encouraged, in order to keep the atmosphere calm, to build supportive relationships, and to ensure homework help is very focused. If more Y7 or Y8 pupils wish to attend later in the school year and they will clearly benefit from the experience, then we usually manage to accommodate them.

On arriving at the club, the teacher in charge usually talks to the children about the homework each child has to do and then helps them to set priorities. Students are encouraged to help each other and the LSA and library staff give support with resources or one-to-one help (for example help with planning a piece of work, finding resources for a research homework, or reading through a worksheet). If students finish their homework they can read, use the Internet, or play a variety of educational board games/puzzles that the club has purchased. Parents either collect their children from school after the club, or students make their own way home if they live nearby in the village. Some other NOF schemes include transport, depending on the grants available.

Evaluation of the club's success is completed regularly and submitted to the LEA/NOF. The school firmly believes in the club and its achievements. Students complete homework that they may not otherwise do and they have help from supportive adults they would not otherwise get. Attendance is regular and students' comments are positive (for example they tell us they are keen to come, they like the help they receive, and they are disappointed if it is cancelled for any reason), and it helps vulnerable new Y7s to settle in to the school and to work together.

Building relationships

The LRC benefits in that the club brings in students who might not otherwise be very keen LRC users, and builds relationships with them. It also gives us another 'function' or role to play in the school. In addition, it gives us a further way to find out about the topics students are studying. Students who are not very confident in school are happy to come into the LRC because they know us from attending Homework Club. The club helps these students find resources, including ICT, and therefore to become more independent library and Internet users.

Our experience has been positive and the running of the club in the LRC has clearly benefited us. Because it is a focused atmosphere with regular attenders the help that the students receive is targeted and specific.
The Head of Y7 can see the organisational skills, the motivation and quality of work of individual students improve. If your school is thinking of setting up an Out of School Hours Club, it is definitely worth doing properly with NOF or other funding and with clear objectives/priorities, rather than simply providing an ad hoc 'add-on' to the services already available in the LRC.
If the library simply opens its doors to anyone who comes along, there is a danger that the atmosphere will become less focused as the club will tend to take on the characteristics of a 'child-minding' activity with a little extra adult support, rather than a place of study with specific guidance and support.

Case Study 3
Skills Club at Menzieshill High School, Dundee

Elspeth S. Scott – LRC Co-ordinator, Menzieshill High School, Dundee
11–18 comprehensive, 900 students

In 1997 Dundee City Council launched a Supported Study initiative in all its ten secondary schools, following a pilot scheme which had been run by the Prince's Trust in one of them. Each school was allocated money to develop Supported Study in the way it felt most suitable. I was invited to be on the steering group to set up the scheme in Menzieshill High School.

The group consisted of an Assistant Head Teacher, the Principal Teacher of Learning Support and me. We decided that the most inclusive way we could operate was to base Study Club (as we called it) in the Learning Resources Centre; to involve as wide a range of staff as possible in supporting the sessions; and not to involve Learning Support directly in order to avoid stigmatising pupils who attended. There was a start-up fund available and some of this money was spent on new furnishings for the LRC to create the right kind of welcoming and comfortable working environment. It has succeeded beyond our wildest expectations.

A higher profile

The club began after the October holiday in 1998 and got off to a slow start, but we learned a good deal from our first year. A relaunch at the beginning of our second year, with a new name, a higher profile and the introduction of practical sessions in P.E., music and art proved successful and by the beginning of session 2000–2001 we had pupils arriving literally on the first day of the new school year wanting to know if Skills Club (as we now called it) was meeting that night.

We have now settled down into a steady pattern. From our small beginnings we have grown to a club with over 100 members and a regular attendance of about forty at each session. Pupils are mainly from S1–S3 (Y7–Y9) with a smaller number of S4 (Y10). Skills Club meets three times a week in the LRC on Tuesdays, Wednesdays and Thursdays from 3.40pm until 5.00pm. Pupils can sign up for one, two or three sessions in the week and they are expected to make a commitment to regular attendance on the nights that they have selected. Each night has its own three regular tutors so pupils know what specific subject help will be available. For example on Tuesdays Mr Sinclair will be there to provide help with maths.

Each session of Skills Club follows a regular pattern. Pupils arrive at the end of the school day, when a subsidised snack (healthy options, of course!) is available. They have ten minutes to socialise and relax and then register and set their targets for the session. All targets are SMART targets: Specific, Measurable, Achievable, Realistic and Time-Bound. This is followed by a few minutes of Brain Gym to make a definite break and get the brains working well and then pupils settle down to steady work on their targets. Many of the pupils use this as an opportunity to do homework making use of the help available; others use it for extra coaching from the attending tutors. Skills Club has purchased materials on study skills and techniques as well as subject specific material. Departments have also been encouraged to provide targeted support materials and extension work. Of course, pupils also have access to all the usual LRC resources and have opportunities for working on topics of their own choice and developing skills and strategies for studying and learning. We have also built up a bank of multimedia resources which enable pupils to develop skills using different learning styles and at their own pace.

In parallel with these general sessions, we run a programme of subject-specific sessions aimed at senior pupils. Each department is allocated ten hours at the beginning of the session and they can decide for themselves when in the academic year they wish to offer these hours. These are usually tied to significant dates in the curriculum, for example coursework deadlines. Any hours not taken up by a department are re-allocated. These sessions take place in the departments rather than the LRC and my only role is to publicise them as widely as possible.

We have also organised a range of extra activities for Skills Club members aimed at developing learning skills. We have done some work on different learning styles and run sessions on developing specific skills, for example memory techniques; we have had a very successful annual residential course involving team building and problem solving; we provided the school display at the Dundee City 'Success Stories' exhibition; and we have had courses from external providers such as Jenny Maddern and The Learning Game.

The role of the librarian

Dundee employs its LRC Co-ordinators as Supported Study tutors in exactly the same way as teaching staff, which means we had to apply and be interviewed in the same way. (It also means we are paid in the same way too.) The difference is that our subject specialism is learning skills and information handling. All the tutors are expected to act as 'facilitating adults': to support and encourage pupils to achieve and to provide specific teaching input when required.

As the one consistent member of the steering group from the beginning, and because the LRC is at the heart of learning in the school, I also have additional responsibilities. I am the main point of contact for pupils; I organise and co-ordinate membership application forms; and I publicise the club, for example at parents' evenings. I am also responsible for organising, and to a lesser extent selecting and ordering, resources to meet the needs of the club.

Into the future

All organisations grow and change in response to changes in the environment. The description above relates to session 2001–2002. In 2002 Dundee decided to create permanent posts of School Co-ordinator for Raising Achievement with Supported Study as part of the remit and the Scottish Executive published new National Priorities for Education. The last year has been one of change for Skills Club and next session will see a new pattern of Supported Study emerging. But whatever form it takes, the aim is always the same: to provide the facilities, resources, staff support and ethos to enable pupils to reach their full potential.

Eileen Armstrong – LRC Manager at Cramlington Community High School,
Cramlington, Northumberland
14–19 comprehensive, 1500 students

In the beginning

The out of hours learning activity programme at Cramlington has evolved organically, by accident rather than design, but always in response to user demand, which perhaps explains its variety and success. Having an average intake and catchment area in national terms Cramlington, in spite of being a leading edge school, did not meet the criteria for any of the externally available funding pots for Study Support – Education Action Zone, Education Extra, Kellogg's Breakfast Clubs, Reading Is Fundamental, Excellence in Cities, etc. And initially all activity was necessarily resourced from the LRC budget or by extra in-school bids. However, creating the right environment and atmosphere for out of hours learning and measuring and demonstrating the impact of the activities on student achievement and attitudes to learning – both formal and informal – has led to the majority of projects now being supported both financially and with extra staffing – by the Community Education Department financed through the County Council.

Research has shown that students who take part in out of hours learning do better in life since those activities are voluntary and require a high level of responsibility, engagement, stickability and teamwork enabling students to learn more through experience and imagination than is possible in the classroom. Whatever the activity our aim is always to cultivate those habits and attitudes which 'build learning power' – help young people develop confidence in their ability to learn so that they can learn faster and better in the classroom – and ultimately find it more fun!

Reading groups

Our first venture into out of hours learning 'played safe' with the setting up of a reading group. Open to all year groups, regardless of ability or previous reading experience, we started small but enthusiastic. Drawing up a term-by-term programme in collaboration with the students proved a useful discipline, gave students ownership of the group, demonstrated commitment and attracted funding and ensured that all students benefited from a lively, if exhausting, mix of discussion, book games, reviewing for magazines and newspapers, bookshop buys, author visits both in and out of school, display work, award shadowing, teacher talks, website creation and in-school promotions around national pegs such as World Book Day and National Poetry Day. This gradually evolved into a more measured cross-phase programme ensuring that all students were able to benefit from the widest possible variety of reading experiences throughout their school career while preserving the sanity of the LRC staff – but always mindful of the students' main wish – a space and time to read and lots of brand new books to widen and deepen their reading. Clearly numbers fluctuate from week to week and year to year as the character of the groups changes but the variety of ages sparks lively debate and news of the group spreads by word of mouth. The keener members support and recruit each new intake and all enjoy special privileges; first pick of new additions, refreshments in the LRC and dedicated group collections. Sixth form students have developed an off-shoot group of their own, meeting monthly, but are always keen to help run activities, train new bookweb designers and encourage reader-to-reader interaction. Although we have experimented with meeting times the students themselves prefer an after school session for the calmer atmosphere and undivided attention of the LRC staff it offers. Having sustained the group for a year the Community Education department now funds the group, promotes it through its own after school activity brochure and provides financial remuneration for the LRC Manager.

As is often the case avid readers are keen writers too and it was at the request of the reading group that the creative writing group was born. Largely self-programming they meet after school for word games, writing exercises, to critically read and constructively review each other's work and to develop their own collaborative story. The LRC provides subscriptions to resources such as *Young Writers* magazine, *Writing Review* and *Writers' News*, collects and promotes competition details and compiles a portfolio of work now also published in their own pages on the LRC intranet. That the LRC Manager is by no means an expert in this field but learns alongside the students sends out valuable messages about the nature of learning. While this group dies off and is resurrected according to the composition of the reading group it is important to nurture and celebrate the talents of all students – the LRC is the natural home for learning and should be the focus for encouraging the productive use of free time both within and beyond the confines of the school curriculum.

A similar offshoot of the Reading group developed in response to the perceived reading needs of users. The 'manga men' were a group of largely disaffected boys who regularly spent their lunchtimes huddled over the at-the-time very limited graphic novel collection. Graphic novel reading is by its very nature a largely subversive underground activity but gradually the boys were drawn in, organised themselves to meet regularly, patiently advised the LRC Manager on graphic novel purchasing, attracted new users to the LRC, produced annotated review lists for publishers and designed comic strips and logos for the LRC. Again although the group was comparatively short-lived it made a lasting impact both on the boys themselves and their attitudes to libraries and on their peers who still enjoy their collections years later.

Alternative activities

The Warhammer Fantasy gaming club was another brave and ultimately unimaginably successful attempt to draw in a whole new user group. Taking advantage of a huge national *Lord of the Rings* promotional scheme supported by the Literacy Trust we invited Games Workshop to run a free introductory session in school and identify a committee of older students to manage the club who then made a successful (PowerPoint) bid for start-up funding to senior management, highlighting the cross-curricular benefits, set up their own club rules and levied a small weekly sub for the purchase of new model armies and consumables such as paint and glue.

Community education involvement

Impressed by the students' initiative and enthusiasm in sustaining the club for a year under the supervision of the LRC Manager, Community Education again offered to finance the club, provide extra youth workers and pay the LRC Manager, transport members to inter-school tournaments and organise an annual trip to Warhammer World. Sixth form gamers have set up clubs in two feeder middle schools and recently gained highly sought-after part-time jobs in the local Games Workshop branch. Teaching staff never cease to be amazed at the stickability of the students (for many it is their motivator for staying in school), the improved concentration and social skills, the complex and regular sustained reading of rule books, magazines, graphics and novels it generates and the complicated strategic thinking and mathematical calculations it necessarily involves not to mention the creative model-making and painstakingly detailed painting skills necessary. Indeed the IEPs and statement reviews of more than one student have been influenced by their involvement in the club and the accompanying *White Dwarf* magazine is arguably the most cost-effective and fought-over resource investment in the LRC. The club has increased the feeling of belonging among a traditional non-user group and behaviour as a whole in the LRC is much improved.

The Chess Club was set up as a result of these closer links forged with Community Education. Initially the students who are from all year and ability groups met weekly in the LRC after school to practise for the UK Chess Challenge using sets purchased by Community Education but now play every break and lunchtime – often with impromptu coaching from the teaching staff popping through. Now that the LRC is seen to be open to and responsive to students' needs and interests it is currently also home to robot wars clubs, special effects (building 'sets' and videoediting short movies) and thinking clubs at their request. While not traditional library activities all involve meticulous research using books, magazines and websites available through the LRC, attract new library users and hopefully instil a love of learning for life. It is a delicate balancing act, maintaining a balance between purposeful study and lively creativity and orchestrating an out of hours learning timetable with something for everyone, visual, auditory or kinaesthetic learner. But it raises the profile of the LRC, changes perceptions, builds students' power and potential to learn and re-energises LRC staff too.

LRC assistants

Another popular extra-curricular activity is the LRC Assistants scheme. Advertised widely at the start of each year with its own job description, person spec and application form the positions are much sought after and many of the students are 'promoted' each year to train the new intake who follow a structured training programme, certified at the end of the year for those who complete. Meeting weekly after school for training, tidying, shelving and 'party' creates a feeling of cohesion among the group and ensures that the service offered to staff and students is always of the highest quality. Because the LRC is single-staffed student assistants are responsible for staffing the desk at breaks and lunchtimes on a rota, shelving sections, booking ICT resources, making new resources shelf-ready, answering enquiries from staff and students and recommending good reads. The satisfaction of working with others and making a difference to others' learning seems to encourage the students' own love of reading and independent learning and provides valuable social support and confidence-building for many.

Sixth form supervisors have responsibility for the assistants' training and overdues and oversee the LRC during free periods to allow the LRC Manager to work in Departments, with classes or on a variety of professional tasks, receiving university and job references and end-of-year awards. Celebrating learning is an important part of what we do with regular prize-givings, certificates, good news postcards to parents and parties for all out of hours learning students.

Study support

More traditional study support is also provided in the form of extended evening opening Monday–Thursday with free photocopying paid for from school funds, bookable PCs and one-to-one help from library staff in finding information, print or electronic. Again response to demand is important and at various times in the year subject specific sessions are organised and advertised weekly – often running for a term for longer or simply as 'one-offs'. Science Surgery staffed by a science teacher and the LRC Manager gave students the time and space to work through difficulties or get ahead with revision, earning extra commendations for quality work from the LRC Manager who had observed their research and learning skills development. French Film club with croissants, computer games, target language magazines and newspapers after school made language learning and cultural awareness fun for GCSE and A level language students. We also show popular films on a large interactive whiteboard 'cinema-style' from a bank of videos joint-funded by the Modern Languages department.

Evidence-based self-evaluation and advocacy

Out of hours learning at Cramlington, then, is as varied and variable as the young people who use it, which is as it should be – as individualised as we can make it with something for everyone, to suit every learning style and type of learner as and when they need it. It demands a flexible, though not limitless, budget; a willingness to listen and respond to demand; a noisier atmosphere than perhaps many are used to; a generous time commitment, energy, imagination and enthusiasm; the hiring out of space for others to use and the setting up of new partnerships so that together everyone achieves more – and an endless supply of biscuits! Success can be measured not only in headcounts, attendance registers and target group surveys but in the many magazines, reviews, videos, models, websites, photo albums, diaries of overheard comments and anecdotes or individual success stories collected over the years.

Ongoing publicity and promotion on school websites, LRC intranets, school newspapers, posters displayed everywhere and anywhere, screensavers, annual governors' and inspection reports keeps users interested and impresses stakeholders, guaranteeing future support and expansion. More importantly we have the satisfaction of seeing new users come in and return, new mind and skillsets develop and learning dispositions nurtured creating resilient, resourceful and reflective learners able to learn with and from each other and take control of their own learning – for life.

Case Study 5
The Homework Help Club – Cramlington[43]

Eileen Armstrong – LRC Manager, Cramlington Community High School
Cramlington Public Library
Wednesday evenings 4.30–6.30pm

It provides:
- study space
- guidance/subject help
- photocopying facilities.

Background

- Set up in consultation with the public library staff in conjunction with the CCHS Community Education Department – this helped to relieve pressure on public library staff too.
- The Public Library Service funded targeted 'Homework Collections' of books – reference only.

Promotion

- CCHS students were surveyed to provide appropriate services and facilities.
- CCHS students designed and displayed posters/flyers around the school.
- CCHS Curriculum Support Department targeted specific students and advertised the club to these parents.
- 'Adverts' were placed in the school newsletter and community broadsheets.
- Public library staff produced posters, flyers and bookmarks to direct students to clearly signed collections – a designated Help Point was set up in the library.
- Letters advertising the club were sent to the local partner middle schools to promote the service.

The club at work

- Maximum take up of ten students per session – on a drop-in basis.
- Several regular attenders have emerged.
- Many attenders are middle school students – often accompanied by parents/carers.
- CCHS students seem to prefer to borrow books and work at home or in school rather than in the public library.
- The availability of home computers might influence this choice.

The future

- More publicity needed to ensure take up – particularly targeted at parents.
- Build up a reward/incentive scheme for attendance.
- Use paid sixth formers from CCHS (and perhaps elsewhere) to support/mentor club members at the club and perhaps in their schools – for skills learning, paired reading, curriculum support, etc.

---

[43] Editor's note: since this case study was written the Homework Club has closed. It was a viable, interesting and supportive school and local library partnership model.

Brain Club Evaluation Form

Please let us know what you think so that we can improve things for next session.
Please tick your answer, or write it in the space provided.

Why did you decide to come to the Brain Club?

It sounded interesting	❏
I wanted to learn more	❏
My mum/dad/gran thought it would be a good idea	❏

Another reason (please write in your answer)

_____

_____

_____

_____

Which activities did you enjoy most? (please number these from 1 up, where 1 is what you enjoyed most)

Brain Gym	❏	Origami	❏
Brain Teasers	❏	Memory Games	❏
Working to Music	❏	Relaxing to Music	❏
Three Brains Poster	❏	Shield	❏
Making Brains	❏	Learning Pyramid	❏
The Brain Game	❏	Something else	❏
I didn't like anything	❏		

Can you write down ONE thing you learned? _____

If your High School ran a Brain Club, would you go to it?

Yes ❏   No ❏   Depends ❏

Thank you for filling in this form. Your opinion is appreciated.

CALDERDALE LIBRARIES

Further Reading

ANDREWS, K. *Extra Learning: Out of School Learning and Study Support in Practice* (Kogan Page, 2001) 0 7494 3343 4

The Basic Skills Agency/The Prince's Trust *Promoting Literacy Through Study Support* (The Basic Skills Agency/The Prince's Trust, 1998) 1 85990 078 X

DEVOY, F. 'If we enjoy it, does it mean we're not learning?' in Dubber, G. *The Internet, the Primary School Library and the Independent Learner* (School Library Association, 2002)

DfEE *Extending Opportunity: A National Framework for Study Support* (DfEE, 1999) 0 855 22 755

DfES *The Essential Guide to the Impact of Study Support* (DfES, 2002) DfES Ref. 0218/2002. See also www.qiss.org.uk – *Study Support in Action: 12 Case Studies*

DfES *The Impact of Study Support* (DfES, 2001) DfES Ref. RR273. Available at www.qiss.org.uk

DfES *The Code of Practice for Secondary Schools* (DfES, Revised 2000) 0 86155 2059

DfES *The Study Support Toolkit: Making it Work in Schools* (DfES, 2000) DfES Ref 0163/2000

Education Extra *Succeeding at Study Support: an Evaluation of 12 Model Projects in Primary and Secondary Schools* (Education Extra, 1998)

Education Extra *Outcomes of Out of Hours Learning; a Framework for Analysis* (Education Extra, 2002) Available at www.educationextra.org.uk/publications/publ-free.html

KEYS, W. and MAWSON, C. with MAYCHELL, K. *Out-of-Lesson-Time Learning Activities: Surveys of Headteachers and Pupils* (DfEE Research Report 127, 1999)

KIRWAN, TONY *The Essential Guide to the Impact of Study Support* (QiSS, 2002)

MACBEATH, J. *Learning to Achieve: The Prince's Trust-Action's Study Support Evaluation and Development Project* (The Prince's Trust, 1997)

MACBEATH, J. et al *The Impact of Study Support* (DfES Research Report 273, 2001)

National Mentoring Network *A Guide to Young People Mentoring, What Is It?* (National Mentoring Network, 2002)

North Lanarkshire Council *Summer Literacy School Handbook* (1998) Available from North Lanarkshire Council, Kildonan Street, Coatbridge, ML5 3BT, 01236 812559

OFSTED *Learning Out of Hours: The Quality and Management of Study Support in Secondary Schools* (OFSTED, October 2002, HMI 466) Available at www.ofsted.gov.uk/publications/

The Prince's Trust *Raising the Standard – the Study Support CD-ROM* (The Prince's Trust, 1999)

SHARP, C. with MASON, K. and OSGOOD, J. *Successful Study Support* (Curriculum Management Update, 7–8 May 2000)

Useful Addresses and Websites

Breakfast Club Plus

A partnership between ContinYou and Kellogg's, Breakfast Club Plus is a UK-wide breakfast club network for schools and communities that incorporates:

- an interactive 'Breakfast Club website'
- regional 'Breakfast Club seminars'
- professional development for those delivering breakfast clubs
- development of a 'nutritional standard'
- a comprehensive, regularly updated, funding guide
- monitoring and evaluation tools for measuring impact.

www.educationextra.org.uk/breakfast-clubs

Several useful publications, such as the codes of practice, are available from ContinYou (formerly Education Extra)

17 Old Ford Road

Bethnal Green

London E2 9PL

Tel: 020 8709 9900

www.educationextra.org.uk

On this site there are several useful online publications. For example *Non-participation in Study Support*; *Parent Extra: A Guide to Out-of-School-Hours Learning*; *Top Tips: Bright Ideas for Running Successful Out-of-School-Hours Clubs.*

4Children

Formerly known as Kids' Clubs Network, this charity is dedicated to creating opportunities for children.

www.4children.org.uk

The National Literacy Trust

Swire House

59 Buckingham Gate

London SW1E 6AJ

Tel: 020 7828 2435

Fax: 020 7931 9986

E-mail: contact@literacy.trust.org.uk

www.literacytrust.org.uk

The National Literacy Trust has some excellent pages on out of hours learning/study support. Including 'Background', 'News Update', 'Resources' and 'Database'.

The Quality in Education Centre
University of Strathclyde
Jordanhill Campus
Crawfurd Building
76 Southbrae Drive
Glasgow G13 1PP
Tel: 0141 950 3186
The Quality in Education Centre is part of the Faculty of Education in the University of Strathclyde, Glasgow. Included in its activities is research into education that is interdisciplinary in approach.

Also at the same address:
The Scottish Study Support Network (SSSN)
Tel: 0141 950 3732
Run in partnership between ContinYou and The Quality in Education Centre, The Scottish Study Support Network has been set up to support all those involved in promoting and delivering study support and out of school hours learning in Scotland. It provides support, advice and network contacts, an e-mail discussion group, conferences, a newsletter and publications.
www.sssn.org.uk

Quality in Study Support – QiSS is part of the Centre for Education Leadership and School Improvement, Canterbury Christ Church University College, Kent. It offers a range of services including consultancy, training, research, publications, events and quality assurance schemes to study support providers.
www.qiss.org.uk/

Campaign for Learning
19 Buckingham Street
London WC2N 6EF
Tel: 020 7930 1111
E-mail: campaign@campaign-for-learning.org.uk
The Campaign for Learning started life in 1995 as an RSA (the Royal Society for the encouragement of Arts, Manufacturers and Commerce) initiative and became an independent charity in November 1997. It was created with the sole purpose of championing the cause for lifelong learning.
www.campaign-for-learning.org.uk

Useful Addresses and Websites

The Prince's Trust
18 Park Square East
London NW1 4LH
Tel: 020 7543 1234
The Prince's Trust is a charity aimed at helping disadvantaged young people aged 14–30 to have a better life.
www.princes-trust.org.uk

The Reading Agency
PO Box 96
St Albans
AL1 3WP
E-mail: info@readingagency.org.uk
The Reading Agency is a UK-wide development agency whose main activities are reading programmes and resources, partnership and pilot models, research and advocacy, training, resources for advocacy and promoting reading.
www.readingagency.org.uk

TeacherNet
TeacherNet is run by the Schools Communications Unit within the Department for Education and Skills. It aims to help education professionals get to the information they need quickly and easily.
There are some useful background and case studies on its website:
www.teachernet.gov.uk/teachingandlearning/library/oosh/